DREAM IT
DO IT LOVE IT

Jenni Winter-Leach

W&M

Dream It, Do It, Love It.

Jenni Winter-Leach

First published in March 2022 by WM Publishing

ISBN 978-1-914265-30-3 ebk

ISBN 978-1-914265-31-0 pbk

Disclaimer: *Dream It, Do It, Love It.* is intended for information and education purposes only. This book does not constitute specific legal, financial, health, clinical or commercial advice unique to your situation.

The views and opinions expressed in this book are those of the authors and do not reflect those of the Publisher and Resellers, who accept no responsibility for loss, damage or injury to persons or their belongings as a direct or indirect result of reading this book.

All people mentioned in case studies have been used with permission, and/or have had names, genders, industries and personal details altered to protect client confidentiality.

Contents

Dedication

This book is dedicated to every single person that gave me
the trust and permission, who's brain I've had the opportunity
to learn from and make changes to, in so many ways.
All of these wonderful people have allowed me to learn,
grow and develop the understanding that I share a small amount
of with you in this book.

Then of course there is my incredible husband, Mark.
Who is my rock and without his support, not only this book
but the entire business and community I have had the privilege
to build over the years, would not have been possible at all.

I also owe a huge debt of gratitude to my parents, who finally
realised that horses were indeed not a *childhood phase* for me
when I left a corporate job to set up *Flying Changes Mindset*
back in 2014, aged almost 30. They have of course always
supported me in any endeavours and have been there
in the background watching and encouraging me to go
for my own dreams.

I want to send so much love and appreciation to my wider
horsey family consisting of friends, trainers, yard managers
and all the team involved in this totally crazy sport that kept me
as close as possible to sane as I think a horse lover can ever get!

And how can I possibly not thank the one group of beings
who have guided me, taught me, given me the highest highs and
the lows too and without who none of my achievements would
have had any meaning.

So I dedicate this book to the HORSES.

What Riders Are Saying About Jenni Winter-Leach

As I know so well, setbacks are a part of horse riding but sadly too often they stop riders from enjoying their passion to the full or getting back to where they once were. This book brilliantly illustrates how our brain works for and against us and how to harness it to achieve your dreams. It is our obligation as riders, trainers and probably families of riders to familiarise ourselves with these concepts, making it a must read for us all.

Jonty Evans, Olympic Eventer

I met Jenni back in 2018 because I was having issues with competition nerves and I felt an imposter in affiliated dressage (on my ex-eventer). It got so bad that I couldn't perform at all out competing, despite being able to train just fine at home.

Jenni helped me to reset my brain and overcome the fears that were holding me back. We went on to really enjoy our competitions and our results dramatically improved. Now, I'm taking both my ex-eventer and my young homebred mare out and about and enjoying every moment (with some great results in there too)!

Previously I avoided talking to other people at competitions because I felt a fraud and didn't think I was good enough to be there. Since changing my mindset, I've been selected to be in Home International Teams and really enjoyed the whole experience.

Jenni knows exactly what is happening in our brains and how to change it too.

I was blown away with the effect she had not only on my riding but on my entire life.

She just understands how brains work for and against us and what we can do to change that. I'm a vet physio and so I'm used to the science of bodies, and I was sceptical at first as I've never had help with anything like this. Jenni just makes it all plain and simple with no jargon and real actionable steps to take away and do, which make lasting changes.

Jenni will always be an invaluable part of my support team as a rider and I'm so excited that she has finally written a book. Although I know this only shares a fraction of her in-depth knowledge, it is a great start for anyone wanting to understand their mind.

Nicky Allen, Client

Welcome

This book is for people who love horses and horse riding. And falling in love with horse riding again especially if you have what I call a challenging horse-riding experience that has impacted you as a rider and taken the joy, the fun and love of horse riding.

Specifically, how you can dream it, do it, love it, which is how you can overcome your riding mindset challenges without having to spend countless hours in lessons.

Many of us think that the way to overcome a problem in our brain is to just keep doing something and it will get better. But you're going to be understanding why that's not the case. In fact, why doing that will only mean it will get worse.

We're going to be looking at relevant theory and some practical things that you can do to overcome any riding mindset challenges.

In most cases I am working with established, competent riders who, for whatever reason, have experienced a loss in confidence with their riding. Maybe you fell or were thrown from a horse. Maybe you had an experience where the horse was startled, or bolted and you suddenly felt the horse was out of control or you had lost control of the horse. And in some cases you had a traumatic accident while riding.

In any case you want to overcome those experiences. You want to regain your confidence as a rider.

We're going to be looking at beliefs.

We're going to be looking what fears are.

We're going to be looking at what dreams are.

We're going to be understanding more how your brain works with you and how it actually can work against you, weirdly enough, as well.

We're going to be helping you to understand how you can work with your brain, which is quite handy.

And then, obviously, we're going to explore some actions that you can take to start creating your own version of success, whatever that might be.

My Promise To You

I promise, I'm going to help you to change the way you think about riding. By the end of this book, something in you will have changed. It may only be tiny, but it will, there'll be something that has helped to change the way that you think about riding.

You're going to update a little bit how you feel about your riding and your goals as well. We're going to have a bit of thinking and a bit of feeling.

And then also you're going to have some tools and steps to put into action.

And you are going to need to participate all the way through this book.

Now, if you're sitting there thinking, Oh, I thought I was just going to read this book … and I'll just take it in and suddenly things will change… then I'm really sorry. You're probably better off using the time to go and watch a movie or the telly or do something else. You need to lean in. Engage.

I'm going to challenge you to is think, feel, and do all the way through this book. What you need to be able to do to make changes go and take action. There is no magic wand. I always say mine is broken.

And in actual fact, what you need to do is process and take in what you're going to hear about and then go and put some stuff into action. Now, like with everything, not everything works for everyone, but something will work for you.

Those are my promises to you.

Are you 100% on board with that?

If you are thinking, *Do you know what, by the end of this I'm going to go away... I'm going to take some action... I'm actually going to do something different...* then we are off to a good start.

Are you thinking, Yes, I want to take some action. I want something to change. That's why I'm reading this book. So yes, I'm going to lean in.

If that's you, then fabulous.

Who Am I?

You might be sitting here thinking who is this woman that is chattering on to me right now? Who is it that's telling me I've got to do things and take action and change by the end of the book.

My name is Jenni Winter-Leach. I am the founder of *Flying Changes Mindset.*

And just to help you understand a little bit about me and how I've come to be here talking to you, I'm going to tell you a bit of a story.

It starts back in 1988, when I was four years old. We are out for a family walk one day, and there I am, stood staring up into the eyes of the most beautiful thing I've ever seen in my life, which is the face of a gorgeous grey horse.

And as I touch his muzzle as he leans over the fence, I feel the softest thing I've ever felt in my life.

And I look into his eyes, and I think, I need to be around you. And I'm four years old, I'm not from a horsey background. I don't have a horsey family, whatsoever. But there is just something in me in this moment that connects me with horses.

Which meant from that moment on, I just knew they had to be in my life.

Now fast forward a few more years to seven years old. When I was allowed to go to a riding school every two weeks, and my parents would take me. I had begged them for years and they eventually gave in on my seventh birthday. They were non-horsey, and they didn't have the resources to buy me horses or in any way really involve me in the sport.

By ten years old, I was at a riding school helping out every other Sunday, where you can imagine, can't you, that someone who turns up every other Sunday – and they don't arrive early either –because my parents wanted a Sunday lie-in (I totally understand why now!). My parents were doing the very best they could to support me in something they knew nothing about, and neither did I, really.

But at the time, I was bullied. I was so badly bullied in that yard – and not just by the other kids – but by the instructors and the yard managers to who now I know were very young themselves, but at the time, they were the adults to me. That meant everything. That meant me being around these horses. That meant me understanding and being confident with them. And that was stripped away from me at ten years old.

My dream, my passion turned sour. I woke up one day and I just remember thinking to myself, at ten, *I can't do this anymore.*

I said to my parents, *Please don't take me to the yard today. I can't cope with it anymore. I don't want to be there.*

And of course, they were OK about it because it meant a lot less time and effort for them not having to take me to the yard. But for me a little bit inside of me died.

That little piece of me, that I'd known since I was four years old; needing to be around these animals – that died. I knew that this

14

wasn't ever going to be a long-term thing. But it wasn't the right time or place for me.

So fast forward quite a few years where I've managed to beg, steal and borrow a few rides here and there and still never had my own horse, until I graduated university, having been told, *there's no money in horses – go and get yourself a proper job.*

I got my degree and when I graduated and started work I had some money. So I went and bought a horse. *(Well, I've never had any since!)*

But that was the beginning of my actual riding life.

There were many years of trying all sorts of different disciplines and different sports… and competing… and qualifying into various championships and… whilst I was simultaneously progressing in a corporate career.

I got to twenty-eight years of age and had been promoted to a global consultancy role in a massive global telecoms firm. I was at the pinnacle of my career – or headed right towards it – but the problem was, I was so out of alignment with my values and what was important to me.

Every time I went and rode my horse – and at this point was on full livery – she didn't want to be around me. She was grumpy. And every time I went and competed in dressage, my scores were getting worse, not better.

I couldn't really understand why until one day, somebody helped me realise that it was because I was burning out in that job. I hated the job. It wasn't in line with what was important to me.

And more importantly, it wasn't in line with what I absolutely loved and adored, which were these four-legged beasts.

Now, having been told for my entire life, *there's no money in horses, make sure you have a proper job* by people who actually just didn't really know or understand my passion, they were somewhat shocked, I have to say, when I turned around to them at age twenty-nine, and said, *I'm leaving my corporate job, and I'm setting up a business to help other horse riders to love and enjoy their sport and feel confident and happy and accepted.*

Now you can imagine the reaction that I got from my friends and family, when I told them I was going to leave a very well paid corporate job and that I was going to – as they put it – *go play with ponies.*

That wasn't actually what I was doing at all.

I set up *Flying Changes Mindset,* which I've now been doing for nine years. Today it has grown it to the UK's biggest equestrian mindset training and coaching company.

And, I am still fueled by my passion.

It's led me to be able to do all sorts of unbelievable and incredible things. I've been able to visit some amazing places, do some amazing things and help some unbelievable people, riders from grassroots all the way up to elite professional riders.

But the people I love working with the most are grassroots riders. People who work hard for this as a hobby. People who really, really want it.

Now, I'm not saying elite riders don't – of course they do. But less of the professionals – and I do absolutely work with professionals – but more of the people that just really want to enjoy the hobby, the passion, that they work and put time, and money, and effort, and energy into and they want to get back what they feel they're putting in.

I've now appeared in all of the major publications. I've been on all of the major media streams. I've been on *Horse & Country* TV a couple of times now – admittedly one where I was dressed as a drag queen in dressage to music – however – but the second time was doing some live demonstrations and talks about rider mindset.

I've also spoken at prestigious events like the *Horse Of The Year Show*, and I was scheduled to go and speak at things like Olympia until the pandemic came. And some of you might have seen me doing Facebook lives, whilst walking with my dog 'The Spru'.

Just in case, you're wondering what that is that I'm doing with a gate on top of a horse. That's the chosen sport that I'm currently doing at the moment. It is called *Working Equitation* and I'm currently on the Team GB Development Squads at the time of press.

But, I get it. I've competed. I have trained. And I have put my life and soul into this sport. And I get the fact that you want to enjoy it. You want to feel successful. You want to feel like you're achieving something and you want to feel like you're progressing.

But there's this part of us that can get in the way.

Sometimes it's our body. But most of the time, the thing that gets in the way, is our brain. And that's what you and I are going to be looking into throughout this book.

Why Do I Do What I Do?

My dream is for my horse to be happy in whatever we do. I didn't share with you at the beginning what my mission is. My mission is the reason that I do this, and the reason that I go through all of the difficult stuff in running a business.

I want every horse and rider to be in a happy and successful partnership.

There are lots of people working on that from the horse's perspective and in training the rider's body, too. And I love that. I think that's fantastic. But I quickly realised that your mindset, is often the missing key to being able to really do this stuff.

I'm not saying you don't need skills and knowledge. Of course you do. But you also need the right mindset, or at least an understanding of how it works in order to ultimately, have a nice effect on your horse.

One thing I finally realised when I was stressed and angry and upset and annoyed was that my mare didn't like me. She really didn't like me.

That's why our scores were getting worse. She didn't like it when I would turn up after work, in a hurry, stressed out.

She she didn't want to be with me. I wouldn't say we were in a happy relationship.

I finally realised the difference that my mindset was making to my ability to have a great partnership with my horse. And I want a great partnership with my horse. I'm sure you do, too.

That is what really, really drives me.

My mission is to work with as many people as I possibly can across the globe, so that every horse and rider can be in a happy and successful relationship.

That's what we all want, really.

And I can impact the horses – which are my absolute passion – through horse riders, like you. That's why I do this. That's my dream. It doesn't matter whether it's ever going to be a reality. That's not the point. That is still my dream.

I don't know how I'm going to do it every step of the way. But I do know my next step, my next thing, my next part, and that's part of the reason for this book – to help more people.

Is This For You?

This is for you if:

- You invest time, effort and training, but feel you're not progressing.

- You give loads of support to others but, forget and neglect yourself.

- You're the world's best excuse-maker. You've always got a reason for why you can't do something... or it's not possible for you... or everyone else can but not you...

- You feel stuck, frustrated, annoyed or upset with your riding and you just want to feel like you're progressing or achieving but you feel like you're not.

Now you might feel any of those things listed above, but, the most important part is:

- You are motivated to change, i.e. you want to do something different to get that difference.

That's the most important part. Anything to do with a change in your mindset, you first have to want it; and believe it's possible.

Otherwise this isn't the book for you.

It's Not For You If...

This is not for you if:

- You believe *others can do it... but you can't*. Maybe you can't at this moment in time. But this is not for people who just think, *Oh, I can't do that sort of thing. I'm not going to bother trying.*

- You aren't prepared to look inside yourself for the answers. You're looking outside of yourself. The answers to finding confidence and rediscovering your love of horse riding are *somewhere out there*. They're not. They aren't outside of you.

- You think it must be everyone else's fault, particularly your horses. Or it's your trainers. Or other riders. Or the weather. In any case, you are convinced that someone else or something else is to blame.

- You want it all to be easy. Maybe you think it *should* come easy. In any case, it seems too hard and you don't want to have to work that hard. Sure we all want it to be easy *some* of the time, but it's not always going to be easy *all* of the time.

- Or maybe you just want to have it *now* – right now – but without putting the effort or the work in to make it happen. If you look at anything you've ever achieved in your life, you will have had to put something in... to make it happen. As I like to say, *It takes something special to make something special.*

- Maybe you're the kind of person who thinks new kit will sort this out. (You've probably already tried all the different kit.) Or you're thinking, *If I get the next saddle or the next great bridle or I get the next thing someone endorses, or I try the next bit of fitness or I do the next fad, then it's going to sort it...* but even though that's the case, it's not actually worked. That's a really key sign that it's something to do with you and your mindset.

And, unfortunately, this isn't for you if

- You want a magic wand to fix it. I often say, *My magic wand is broken.* In fact it isn't just broken because I've never had one.

But what I do have is tools, techniques and ways of working with brains that does make rewiring and changes to your brain possible. Sometimes it *feels* like it was a magic wand that fixed it, but it's not.

We know what fixes things. We know what works. What gets you un-stuck. Unblocked.

But then finally, this isn't for you if:

- You've given up on your dreams, you're going through the motions and you're just settling for being unhappy. This isn't fair on you. And it's not fair on your horse.

You *have to* want to change.

Hopefully, I haven't lost you. But, if some of that is you but you are ready to change then it sounds like you are reading the right book!

Does This Sound Like You?

I have a friend and client. Let's call her Jo. Jo is married, has children. She's a one-horse owner and she loves her horse. She has the time and money and is willing to invest the time into her horse. She's diligent. She takes responsibility.

She's a good rider and owner. She does research. She reads. She studies. She does courses.

She rides socially. She is not a professional and she used to compete but not now. Maybe one day she will compete again.

But she had an accident. In fact several.

Now she doesn't believe she is good rider any more. She lacks confidence. She doesn't believe in her self enough. She sets low goals – generally – not just horse riding goals. She has lowered her expectation. She looks to others for support and reassurance and she's perfectly fine, once she gets going, but she limits herself mentally.

She sees other riders doing OK. Riders who've had an accident and recovered. Still riding. Back competing.

She has excuses and rationalisations for why they are OK and why she isn't. She's what we might call the exceptional case. *This works for everyone else but me. I'm the only one who can't...*

It's just me... I'm the only one experiencing this... This will never change...

Secretly, she's a perfectionist. She has to get *everything* right. Everything has to be right before she can be. But she personalises faults and mistakes.

And she wonders, *Why can't I just do this?*

But she did change. It can be fixed.

What Do You Want?

Jo wants to feel and ride confidently, again. She doesn't want to feel fearful. She wants that fixed. She wants to love riding again.

There are a lot of things that will help Jo. If we asked a group of riding experts, I am sure they would all have their opinion on what will help Jo regain her confidence and love horse riding again. There are lots of things you can do that they might suggest. There might be eleven things… or twenty-seven things… or one hundred and five things...

But in my experience of successfully helping riders find their confidence, and rediscover the joy of being on a horse... there are three things that must happen.

First you need to know what you want. You must have a dream. Now instead of a dream, so often I see no dream, no goals, and no vision for horse riding. I see riders like Jo – once competent riders – frustrated, confused, doubtful, fearful, comparing themselves to others… and very clear in what they *don't* want.

Be clear: my program is not just about horse riding. If you think this is just about horse riding you've missed the point. This is how Jo does life! Horse riding is just an metaphor.

So you need a dream.

Secondly, you need a change in mindset. You need a belief in yourself where you can just get on a horse and do it.

Instead of that I see inaction, lack of growth, stories, justifications, lots of talk, blame. They blame their equipment, the horse, the yard, the weather.

And I see limitation, distraction, delays, obstacles and excuses — perfect excuses. And fear, confusion, and comparison.

There's no strategy for moving forward. There's a poor understanding of themself and their horse.

There's a *fixed mindset* where they are not prepared to make mistakes. There's perfect excuses for not taking any action steps. So you need to have a *do it whatever* mindset. Simply put: you need to get on your horse and ride. Often.

And thirdly, you do need to love it. Not just the good bits.

All of it.

The easy rides, the hard rides, the perfect rides, the mistakes, the nice weather, bad weather, your gear — the right gear, the wrong gear, the yard work, the grooming.

And your horse. Especially, the relationship with your horse. Your horse *knows* how you feel. They *know* that you are holding back. They *know* you don't trust yourself or them. And, they also know when you do. You need to cultivate a *growth mindset.*

This book is designed to get you thinking on and off your horse. During and away from horse riding.

And it is designed to get you thinking about life... and what sort of *ride* you want. There is no magic wand.

And there are no perfect rides. *They are all perfect.*

PART I

The Three Steps

Dream It
Do It
Love It

What Will We Cover?

The secret to rediscovering your love of horse riding is a change in mindset. We're going to cover the three key steps that you need to understand to make changes to your mindset.

As I explain the three key steps I'm going to stop and ask you to reflect and make notes. The people who get the biggest changes, sooner, do the written work. So stop and do the activities the whole way through.

Decide. Don't read on unless and until you've attempted the activities. If you skip over the activities you will miss out. You will leave value on the table. If you are in the habit of jumping ahead and skipping important activities then that's probably why your love of horse riding has diminished. That's probably what's wrong with your riding.

That's also why I want you to keep checking in.

And as well as throughout the book, at the end, I'm also going to ask you to reflect on what are your overall insights? What have you got from this? What have you gained?

And what actions are you going to commit to?

Understand this book is about taking baby steps. The research tells us to take baby steps. Incremental gains. If you take too big a step you will lock up. The default position is where you are now. Blocked. Stuck. Anxious. Doubting.

This book is designed to get you thinking. Trying stuff. Little things. Baby steps.

Of course, there is other stuff to try. And yes, some intermediate and advanced stuff. This book is about ground floor, entry level, one step at a time, baby steps stuff.

Foundational techniques and strategies that work.

Of course, if you want more, I will give you several options to learn more or work with me. Paid and free options as well. All of that is at the very end of the book along with a list of links and resources.

But for best results, start here. For best results work through this book in sequence, as advised.

Three Key Steps

There are lots of ways of changing your mindset. I'm sure if we assembled a panel of experts they'd all have their recommendations. But in my experience of successfully working with riders who need to adjust their mindset, I've found three key ideas that deliver those changes sooner.

- Dream it.
- Do it.
- Love it.

The first part, *Dream it,* is all about your awareness.

How aware are you of what you *do* want? You're probably more aware of what you *don't* want. But, how aware are you of what you *do* want?

The next part is all about *Do it*. Funnily enough, this is not just about actions, but it's also about choices and decisions. That's why we will also explore what stops those decisions and actions (a clue – its often fear).

And then, *Love it* – which is all about enjoyment. Why love it?

Because why would you just set a goal, which is dream it, take the actions to do it and then not actually enjoy it?

So these are the three ideas we're going be exploring throughout this book.

- Dream it. Where do you want to be? What you want to be doing?

- Do it. What stops you taking action? What are you going to do to make it happen?

- Love it. Make sure you not only enjoy the destination, but you're enjoying the journey as well.

And they are steps. It's a sequence.

Step 1: Dream It

The first step is *Dream it.*

Now you've probably heard the saying that... *a dream is just a goal without a plan.*

I want to change that saying.

A dream is just a goal without action.

People don't like the word *dream* a lot of the time because they think, *Oh dream? That's things that never happen. That's the stuff we do as children. They are wishes. Why have their dream? Surely, we need to be talking about goals?*

Well dreams are goals. They are just really big ones – unless you just keep dreaming about something and never take any action towards it. And then it *is* a dream.

And you have got options for dreams. You can keep dreaming, you can keep putting lots of thought into something and wishing and hoping, but never doing anything about it. Probably, that is you're putting quite a lot of energy into something that you're never going to do anything about.

And you might *wish* for things like winning the lottery but if you never go and buy the ticket, then it's certainly never going to happen, is it? But note, it only increase your chances *slightly* by buying the ticket.

But also, if you only ever set small goals, and they're never big enough, you'll always be limiting yourself. Or it suggests you are limiting yourself. You are playing small.

So a dream is simply a big, audacious goal.

- What's the thing you'd really *love* to *have?*
- What's the thing you'd really love to do, really love to *be?*
- Where's the place you'd really love to *go?*
- What's the thing you'd really love to *do,* really with your horse?
- What's the thing you've always wanted to experience?

That's dreams. And the thing with those is we can make them happen. I can't make them happen for you, but we can make them happen with you. Importantly, you can make them happen.

What you have to do is understand the process, and then just follow it.

Simple as that. So, what is this process?

The Seven Reasons Why Dreams Fail

But just before I tell you this, I want to explain that all dreams – goals – fail for one of seven reasons. They are:

1. A gap in your information or knowledge.

2. Not adhering to the three fundamental laws, which I'm not covering in this book. (But if you want to know more about, there's an opportunity to find out more in the resource section.)

3. Limiting beliefs.

4. Misaligned values.

5. Incorrectly formatted or designed goals. This is a really common one. This is how most people make goals. They stick a finger to the wind and hope. Or they take someone else's goal on. Or they do it because they feel they should do it. Or they do it because someone told them to. But if it's not the right goal for you, you're never actually going to stand the test of time trying to achieve it. Because by pure nature of it being a goal – and not a thing you're already doing – means you probably need to do some different stuff to get there. And therefore you're going to overcome challenges. And you're going to have to do some learning to get there.

6. No consistent or determined actions. Or no action. Inaction.
   If you don't take any action – like ride your horse, you are highly unlikely to ever win the class.

7. Negative emotions. Importantly, succumbing to negative emotions. Settling for a negative mindset and feelings.

Take a moment right now. Do any of these sound like you? Which ones? How do they show up?

The Goal Setter And Goal Getter

So we need to understand that there are two parts to our brain. And our brain is always operating out of these two parts.

GOAL SETTER

Linear
Sequential

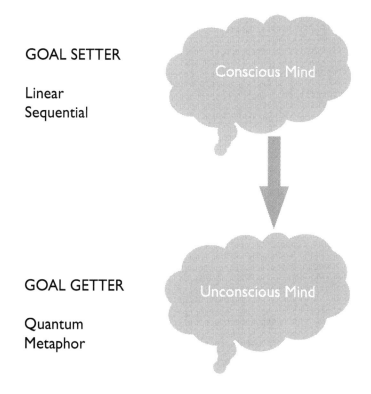

GOAL GETTER

Quantum
Metaphor

The first part is called the **conscious mind**. And this is the part of our mind that works with logic. And this is the part where we have pictures and words – which is what we call thinking. This is the part where we see patterns and process – its very logical.

And it's very sequential. This happens... then this happens... then this happens.

Subsequently, this part of our mind is great for setting goals which is why its sometimes called the **goal setter**.

We need to use both parts of our mind... the right way.

And the way that most people use the conscious mind is the wrong way. And I'll tell you why in a moment.

So what the conscious mind really loves being involved in is what, when, targets and specifics. And this is where we're used to operating.

A lot of people have heard of SMART goals and if you've not heard of them they used a lot in corporate world. A SMART goal is:

- Specific

- Measurable

- Achievable

- Realistic

- Time bound

I have a problem with SMART goals, because who is it that decides if it's achievable or realistic? Just because something hasn't been done before does not mean it's not achievable. Look at the incredible things that have been achieved in the world.

And a classic example of this one is Roger Bannister, who decided he was going to run a mile in under four minutes. At that point in time it hadn't been done. His conscious brain said, *I'm going to do it.*

But his unconscious brain took over the next part.

Everyone told him it's not achievable. It's not realistic. But he had a dream. He decided it *was* achievable and realistic. All he had to work out was how he was going to do it. And at that point, he didn't really know how, but he decided he was going to, anyway.

So, the goal setter – the conscious mind – wanted to know the *what* – run the mile in under four minutes. It didn't know *by when.* I don't know if Bannister set a specific time frame around running the sub four minute mile. But let's say he said, *I'm going to do it within a year.* The target is very clear, and very specific. So specific and measurable.

The timeline aspect is interesting.

Time is difficult – especially with horses. They are sensitive beings, particularly when we put a time frame on them. They tend to cotton-on to the fact that we've got an agenda like a time frame… and then, they'll generally do entirely the opposite.

But for humans, if we don't set a time frame, in our conscious mind, our unconscious has a difficult job.

So we have this second part of our brain – our **unconscious mind**, which they say is doing 80% of the work.

Our unconscious mind is incredibly important. It is the huge part of our brain that we are yet to really, truly understand. But the bits we do know about it is that our unconscious mind is actually the **goal getter.**

It works in what we call quantum or metaphor. It's not linear and sequential.

It's abstract. It loves pictures. It loves metaphor. It loves story. It puts weird and wonderful things together that don't make any sense. It's the part that drives emotion. And it's the part that decides upon action; or not.

Our unconscious mind is concerned with two really important parts of any goal. It will work out the *how*. And it also needs to understand the *why*.

This is why our goals need to be right for us. (We go into what's right for you in real detail in the Mastermind programme, but for now, you know enough.)

But the unconscious mind does look at the *how*. This is why we have to know how to use our brain.

A dream is just a goal without action; and it doesn't actually have to have a plan.

This was a real light bulb for me when I was talking to a fellow Master NLP trainer who is incredibly good at helping people to achieve their dreams. I was very fortunate enough to be able to have spend time with him and ask him a lot of questions about goal setting and goal getting.

I was saying to him, *Look, in sport, we need to develop skills. We need to take action. We do need a plan, especially if we've got a championship we want to qualify for.. or we've got to hit certain deadlines to get certain percentages of certain marks. Or there are certain competitions that we need to get into. We need to have a plan. How can we not have a plan?*

What he said was really great. He said, *I'm not saying don't have a set of actions that you need to take. Just don't have them mapped out and expect it to go that way.*

And a perfect example of this was when I was a graduate project manager.

I was looking after multi-million pound projects in software and hardware, installs and upgrades in the telecoms industry. Big high profile projects. And I was constantly replanning, redoing, working things out, and changing things. I was always trying to keep to the time frame. I was always trying to stick to the scope of what the customer wanted. And always trying to keep it in and on budget. That was my role.

Problem was, of course, it didn't always happen that way.

One of my colleagues – also fresh out of university – couldn't get her head around why the engineers didn't just follow the plan. Why, when she gave them a plan – that she spent a long time doing, and that had been agreed, and that's what they were going to do – did it not just happen? As agreed?

I said to her, *Well, why do you think our job exists as a project manager? Surely, if it was a case of giving them the plan, that's what they would do, and we would be redundant.*

And that blew her brain because she'd never thought of it that way.

And it's exactly the same with sport.

It's about having the actions that we need to take – and some of them may need to happen before and after others – but it's more about having a list of the actions and check have we achieved that one?

- Yes? No?

- What do we need to do to achieve it?

- How can we do that?

- Where do we need to get feedback from?

- What do we need to be learning what's going on?

- What's the next step?

- Am I doing that bit?

And although we may have an idea of certain things we need to achieve, we cannot have a rigid plan. Because apart from anything else, our horses *know* if we have a rigid plan. They *know* if you have an agenda. Have you ever put a plan down and your horse has had a *different* one – for whatever reason?

I am very much going through this at the moment because that lovely horse's bottom that you saw in the photo, earlier, is the bottom of a 17.1hh Irish sports horse... trying to do a sport that really, at the upper levels, is designed for small compact, and agile horses like Iberians, which is what the most of the sport consists of – it originated in Spain and Portugal, too.

Now, you can absolutely do this sport on other breeds of horses, but my boy is definitely not optimally designed to perform that way. Everything's a little bit too low down and a little bit too narrow. And you need sort of compact, bouncy horses. He's not that. He's designed for straight line galloping and jumping, *and* that's what he loves too.

He doesn't want to go to advance with me, funnily enough, *and* has made his thoughts on this very clear. I'm having to change – because it is my dream to ride for Team GB – but I'm having to change the actions I'm taking to get there.

Now, it was definitely never in my plan to not actually do it on my boy. But I have to accept that we need the right tools for our discipline and whilst it pains me to consider him a *tool,* that is the fact of it in our sport. We have to have a capable and willing partner. He is sadly a square peg in a round hole, especially when we consider him for the Advanced levels.

Part of my actions that I'm having to take are listen to the feedback, work with it and actually source myself a horse that is more aligned with the goal.

Do you agree with me?

You lay a plan down and your horse almost gets wind of it and they go? *No, we're not going to do that.*

We can't set a rigid plan, but we can have a series of actions that we want to take.

Because what our unconscious mind is really good at doing is figuring stuff out. It's really good at being creative. It's really good at coming up with the answers to problems.

And here's the other bit that it's really good at.

It's a bit like Google. When you type a question into Google, it gives you the answers. And your unconscious mind is just the same.

It doesn't like things that are *unresolved*.

Have you ever had a situation where you've perhaps been doing a pub quiz, or someone's asked you a question, and you *know* the answer. It's at the tip of your tongue, but it won't come and it's really annoying. And then you have to let it go because you've got to move on to the next question. And later, you're in bed, or you wake up the next morning, or you're in the shower, or you're driving somewhere, or you're washing the dishes – whatever –and suddenly you go, *Bob Dylan!* And you think, *Where did that come from? I wasn't even thinking about the question at that point in time.*

But your unconscious mind found the answer and gave it to you.

That's because there's something called the Zeigarnik Effect – loops that exist in the unconscious mind. (You don't need to worry about what they're called, I just think it's a cool name.)

What that means is, once you open a loop, once you ask a question, your unconscious mind has to go and find an answer and give it to you.

And then the conscious mind decides whether or not it's happy with it.

And this is where we have to be really careful. Because the questions that we ask ourselves are the questions the unconscious mind is going to answer. Reread that last sentence.

So if we ask ourselves:

- Why am I no good at this?

- Why is everyone else better than me?

- Why do they find it easy?

- Why do I find this so hard?

- Why is it so difficult?

Guess what your unconscious mind is going to go and do next? Right. It's going to go off and find you all of the evidence and the answers to all of those questions.

That's why the first thing that you need to start doing is asking yourself better questions. Questions that require better answers. More resourceful answers. Rather than ask, *Why can't I...?* ask instead, *How can I...?*

So if you're asking yourself:

- What do I need to find out about this?

- What do I not know that I'm going to find?

- What am I OK with?

- What can I be doing to get better?

- Who do I know that might be able to help me?

- What information can I go and source?

- What exactly is it that I need to improve upon?

Those are helpful questions. They're great coaching questions as well, because they go and allow the search that goes on in your unconscious mind to happen in a really positive way.

They help you to set the unconscious mind off, funnily enough. So although you think at the moment that you're taking this in all very logically… and you're making sense of it… and you feel like you're even listening to my voice… and you might even be taking notes…

… what's really going on is your unconscious mind is going, *Oh, so that's a bit related to that then, isn't it? Oh, I think that might be about this at all. I don't really understand that. That doesn't make any sense. But that does. Ah, yes, no, that makes total sense. Now that's OK, I understand that…* that's what's really going on in your brain.

We're only using a tiny, tiny part. It's called our prefrontal cortex. That's the part we actually use for conscious thought, and the logical stuff.

This is why you can achieve your riding goals without having to spend hours and hours in the saddle, in lessons.

This is actually proven. Riding, learning or learning about riding really occurs when you're off the horse.

So although you're having your lesson, and you're taking it in, and you're processing it, and you're doing all this stuff, and you're trying to realign things and do things and change stuff, and do whatever your coach or your instructor is telling you in your lesson, actually, when you get off the horse, that's when the conscious mind is no longer occupied with doing stuff, trying to get it right – because the conscious mind is occupied with the here and now, right? – and what's going on is the unconscious mind starts doing its thing.

It starts going away and thinking about what might be happening, what might be going on. It starts to put things together. It starts to make linkages. It starts to play about with things in your body.

That's how it works.

Because, although riding obviously is a *physical* thing – and *physically* we need to be able to do the job – we really only need a few things for good riding.

An amazing guy that I am very privileged to spend time with and learn from is a man called Clive Milkins. He is the Technical Manager for the Canadian Paralympics Dressage Team, and he's also the guy that was the coach of Sophie Christiansen who won triple gold, at the London Paralympics.

And he always says, *You only need three things to ride with.* You need a head with a brain in it; a torso; and ideally something to sit on. And even then – *even then* he says – *even that could be prosthetic*, because he knows people with prosthetic bottom cheek, for instance.

So if you only need a head with a brain in it, and a torso functioning, obviously you need to be alive to ride, then why do we get so bogged down with all the other stuff? And that is because our conscious mind is occupied with all the other stuff.

When you set a goal, what's really common – and I find this with a lot in clients – is when I ask, *What do you want?* they will tell me all the things they *don't* want.

Their goals sound a bit like, *I would like to ride a show jumping round without falling off.* And you think that would be a good goal, wouldn't you? And I'd agree. I totally understand why you'd want that as a goal.

The issue is that what the brain hears is: *fall off.* It forgets the first bit – ride a show jumping round – because all it's thinking is: *fall off, fall off, fall off.*

And funnily enough, what happens when we are riding, is we are seeing images – pictures, movies – of *falling off and everything* that goes with falling off. And our body gets ready for falling off. And funnily enough, because our body is ready for falling off, we're then giving those cues to our body – priming our body – which goes, *Oh, yeah, OK, falling off, I'm ready for that one.*

And then your horse stops or jumps a huge jump or lands and disappears off... and you fall off. And our horses are picking up on this stuff as well through your micro or gross movement. And so they react accordingly, too.

We need to allow our unconscious to do more things. But a lot of the time, we're not letting it do that job. A lot of the time, we're still too involved in the what, when, target specifics, the linear sequential stuff, and we're not allowing our unconscious mind to come up the *how* and the *why*.

When Things Don't Go As Planned

When we set a goal, and we put a plan in place, and we expect it to go that way – and it doesn't – two things happen.

One, we can get really frustrated that it's not going the way we want to... which then starts to makes us feel bad... which then starts to make us beat ourselves up... which then starts to make us ask unhelpful questions... which then starts to make us feel bad...

... and so on and so forth. And the cycle begins again. We are on rinse and repeat!

The second thing is, the unconscious mind is still working stuff out. It's not necessarily as fast as the logical brain. The unconscious mind is incredibly fast – but it doesn't always give us the answer we want to hear, or the thing we want to know, when we want it. So the pub quiz answer arrives at 2 am! It can take its time to go and find the answer... and then it gives it to us... but not always at the time we've asked it to.

So if you set a goal, for say, three months time, and you feel you're taking actions and you're working towards it; Let's say you've got this plan of, *I'm going to do step A... which goes to B... which goes to C... which goes to D and eventually I'll get to M.*

And you're taking the action − A,B,C − and that's all fine, but then D is not happening for some reason. So now you're starting to get frustrated. You don't go on to E. Or you don't go to F and then you get annoyed, because you've got to go back to A, B and C − *again* − to try and get to E... but you're not getting there.

And now it's two months in and you're thinking, *For goodness sakes, I've got a month left of my three months goal, and I've only done A, B and C and I'm trying to get to M.*

And you get *more* annoyed and frustrated.

Even though your unconscious mind is fully aware of where you're at, and where you need to get to − particularly if it's got the information in front of it − it will go and sort out the *how* because that's its job.

It might be that actually, it's two months and twenty-nine days − so, just a day to go − before you actually want to achieve the thing you're going to achieve. And suddenly, the unconscious mind is able to piece together all of the different learning and all of the different stuff... and it just clicks.

But if you'd given up earlier, when you've done two months, and you decided it wasn't good enough, it wasn't going to happen, or you changed your goal, or you gave up on it, you haven't given your unconscious mind the time it needed to come up with all of the *how.*

And the only way it comes up with the how is to continuously assess, and to allow it to go and search for the answers to those assessments.

We do need a time frame to be aiming at but we may actually need to move that time out a bit if we don't make it, because of factors outside of our control.

Or because we have learnt something new that needs some attention. Or because we underestimated the learning required to make it happen in that time frame. And that's OK too.

Just reset the time frame and go towards that new one. *Just keep assessing and adjusting.*

So I'm just going to pause for a moment.

I want you to put any thoughts or insights that you might have in the space provided below so that you can just check in where you're at, so far.

Is this making sense? Do you have any questions? Or insights? What are your thoughts on this?

I recently ran a live workshop and asked delegates to put their comments into the chat. Here's some very common feedback. Maybe you've had similar insights.

- I'm definitely asking the wrong questions. I always ask myself, *Why am I not good enough?* I'm definitely now going to ask what I need to work on to get better.

Really common. But it makes such a difference. And actually, what we're looking at here is the fundamental difference between what Professor of Psychology at Stanford University, USA, Carol Dweck calls a *growth mindset* and a *fixed mindset.*

A *fixed mindset* is worried about feedback. You're worried about getting it wrong. How you will look – to others. Being perfect. Getting it right the first time you try something.

And you're asking yourself those negatively skewed questions and getting those unresourceful, unhelpful answers.

A *growth mindset* is much more about cultivating skills, attitudes, capabilities. And asking more resourceful questions like, *Where do I find this information? How can I work that out? What do I do with this feedback? What's this all about for me? How do I grow from this?*

Importantly, you need to listen to the questions you are asking yourself.

Here's another common insight.

- Does the horse's conscious and unconscious mind work in a similar way? Will their unconscious mind also figure things out after schooling lesson?

Great question, right?

It's worth knowing that a horse's brain and a human brain are physically different. Horses have a very tiny prefrontal cortex. If you put your hand on your forehead, the prefrontal cortex sits right there at the front, inside your skull.

The prefrontal cortex – is the part of our brain that humans use for all this logical stuff. Whereas horses don't really have a large prefrontal cortex. They have a tiny bit of it, which is why we can train them. They do have some capacity for *thinking*, but mostly they learn through association, which is all the unconscious mind stuff, linkages, association, x equals y and z. That's why we have to be really careful about training methods with the horse. Horses make rapid associations.

But a horse's unconscious mind absolutely goes and figures out the stuff after a training session.

If anyone's ever had a young horse, and they teach it something, and then they go away for a few days, when they come back, that young horse hasn't lost that learning. Often it's even better, even though you haven't been drilling into them for the last few days.

The unconscious mind really works in pictures and emotions, whereas the conscious mind tends to work more in logic, sequences, diagrams or words or even seeing the words.

The horse's unconscious mind is constantly working in the pictures and associations. Of course, a horse is going to create those pictures and sort through stories in a slightly different way to humans. (We don't really know exactly how it works, obviously, because we can't actually speak to a horse the way we would a human.) A horse makes those linkages and because it's unconscious, the horse isn't controlling how that happens. It's just happening. Horses are fantastic at living in the moment because their brains are just wired that way.

This is why dreaming is really important.

If we set something out there, we don't have to know *how* we're going to get there. Most dreams are squashed because people don't know *how* and if they don't know how something will happen the dream gets squashed.

It doesn't matter how. First dream it.

If it's something you really want; and you are prepared to do whatever it takes to get there; and you're OK with the fact that there's going to be challenge and accept that there may be some tough decisions and difficulty – because there will be – set the dream, anyway – the *what* – and then allow the unconscious to work out the *how*.

You can only ever work out how with the information you've got... in this moment. So all you really need to do is: know the first step.

Dream it.

Everyone who dreams of winning the lottery buys the lottery ticket. They don't know *how* the lottery works; but incredibly, they just trust if they buy the ticket, there is a possibility it just *might* happen.

Now, I'm not saying that getting somewhere with your horse is like buying a lottery ticket. I am not saying that by just saying it you're going to do it or that it will happen. Obviously, you've got to put a lot more effort and action.

But you don't have to know or have mapped out the entire thing. Just keep focusing on the dream; the goal and taking the next step.

You've got to know what it is you want; and roughly when it is you want it.

Even within that you might need to flex a little bit.

If you want to achieve something you may still find that your horse doesn't or isn't capable of doing what you want.

You then need to consider, *What's more important to me? Achieving this with my specific horse, or achieving the outcome?*

If achieving it is more important, you might need to consider whether you're in the right partnership with the current horse and whether decisions need to be made about your horse in order for you to achieve the goal. And if your horse is the most important thing, you might have to adjust the goal to fit in with your horse.

But you don't exactly have to know *how* you're going to get there.

Once again, any other thoughts or questions on this one? I'm sure you've got questions or thoughts or insights. Please take a moment to write them down before we move on.

Here's some common feedback I received in live workshops.

- I really enjoy working out the challenge, because our horse can't communicate. We have to keep working out the way forward to reach our goals. But it can definitely be a frustrating process.

Yes, it absolutely can. And I'm not saying to *dream it, do it, love it* like it's going to be easy. What I'm saying is *dream it.* The *doing it* part involves frustration, annoyance, difficulty, challenge, questioning – of course it does. It involves all of those things. Factor that in.

With regards to achievements, a lot of times it's like pushing water uphill. It's really, really hard. And then, just as you get to the top, you think, *I can't do it anymore, it's just not happening.* And then you give up and all the water runs back down the hill again. Then you are back at square one and you have to start again with all the effort.

So you've got to keep pushing until you get to that little brow of the hill, and then the water runs down the other side as planned. It becomes a lot easier.

It's the same principle for me with regards to training.

Ultimately, though, you have to make sure that the goal you are setting is something you not only will love when you've achieved it, but will you love it as you're doing the journey to get to it? And that's not to say all the time.

There will be questions. How many of us horse lovers question our sanity when it's cold and dark? When it's rainy and wet? At those times we just think, *What am I doing?* Will we have to get up stupidly early to go and compete, or we get home ridiculously late? Or when we look at our bank account and realise that we're on beans, again?

So, yes, there are challenges. Of course there are.

What ultimately keeps us going is that little four year old girl who looked up at that grey horse and thought, *I need to be around you.*

That is the part of me – the unconscious part that has become conscious – that drives me.

- People often tell me at this point, I always allow and expect my horse to process new things but I haven't allowed myself the same luxury.

I love that insight. That's brilliant. We have to allow ourselves time to process new things. We have to give ourselves the time and space to do that. That's really important.

- I'm now glad I'm giving my unconscious mind a chance to figure out my younger mare. I thought I'd like to quit many times, but each time I nearly quit, I learned more about the process and trying to be friends and not quitting on her.

Amazing. I love that, too. 100%. Again, you have to give yourself time. Sometimes we have to take the pressure off... in order to actually achieve more. We have to go slow... to speed up.

DREAM IT DO IT LOVE IT

What Kills Most Dreams?

What kills most dreams? Straight up: Fear. Fear is the biggest killer of dreams out there. It isn't the fact that it's difficult or it's hard. It isn't the fact that we aren't prepared to put in the work. It isn't anything like that. It is fear, especially if we don't even dream or set goals in the first place.

Right now, have you been thinking, *There's something I'd really love to do… but there's fear in the way? I'm not even going to contemplate the possibility of it. I'm just going to ignore it and hope it goes away.*

Fear is the issue if:

- You've stopped yourself doing something in the past because of fear…

- You've stopped yourself setting a goal because of fear…

- There's something you've always really wanted to do, but you're not doing it because of fear…

It could be the fear of the change required to get there. It could be the fear of not having the resources like the time or the money to get there. It could be the fear of not having the support to get there. No surprises here.

Overcoming fear, really is all in your head. What I do want you to understand is that fear is the main killer of dreams, because it stops action, and it stops action for a reason.

Fear is caused by all sorts of things.

- Fear is caused by trauma.

- Fear is caused by not feeling good enough in comparison.

- Fear is caused by not feeling like we are good enough and we're going to get found out.

- Fear is caused by not actually having the skills in the moment. And being worried that you won't cope.

- Fear is caused by things like overwhelm where it's all too much, and we don't know how to deal with it.

They're the most common things that we feel fear to.

Why am I showing you a picture of a tiger?

The above picture might already be causing you to feel fear.

The most interesting part is that it elicited an emotion or a feeling in you just by looking at it.

If not, that's fine.

In any case, fear is there to protect us. It is there to keep us alive. And you know what? Well done. You've done a good job, because if you are still reading this, you have survived 100% of everything you've been through right up to today. You're still here.

Your brain is doing something right. It's working. It kept you alive. It might be irritating you. It might be frustrating you. It might be annoying you. It might be upsetting you, but it's made you safe and kept you alive, because here you are.

We're only ever born with two fears – a fear of loud noises; and a fear of falling.

Babies have a fear of loud noises. When they hear a loud noise they jump! Its called the startle response. We need to check out what that loud noise was and see if it was danger or not.

All babies have that fear. If you startle a baby it will normally cry. But we get over that one. Later, loud noises might make us jump, but we're not generally fearful of a loud noise. We normalise a noisy world.

And we have a fear of falling. You don't really want to be falling off things.

But again, we get over that. If you've ridden a horse you got over that. Now we know there is a danger we *might* fall off and there are some people – non-horse riders – that do have a fear that they might fall off. That's understandable. But if you've been a horse rider, it's illogical especially because you chose to get on that horse. If you genuinely thought it was 100% going to happen, every time, then you would not be a horse rider.

For long.

Many times I thought about giving up horse riding after a fall. I've contemplated doing crocheting instead, but I'm still convinced I'll probably end up stabbing myself with a crochet needle.

So I decided, you know what? I might as well do the thing I enjoy instead.

So fear really is all in your head. It's in your mind. But here's the deal; it's in the unconscious mind. The bit we are aware of is the consequence of fear, which is in the conscious mind.

How Your Brain Handles Fear

This is an MRI scan of one brain - *the same brain* – but in two different states. An MRI scan basically is a heat map showing the allocation of blood throughout the brain. Just so you know you are looking down at the top of someones head.

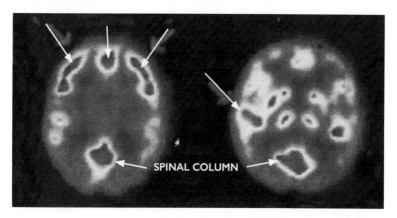

SPINAL COLUMN

The two large blobby circles at the bottom of each head – in both images – is the spinal column. The spinal column always lights up on an MRI scan because it has a constant flow of blood even when we lie still.

The top of both heads, is the prefrontal cortex. The one on the left shows increased blood flow in the prefrontal cortex region; the one on the right decreased blood flow.

The brain on the left-hand side is a brain at rest. The person was in the MRI scanner just resting, maybe *thinking* about things, maybe day dreaming, for example. You'll see three elongated shapes in the prefrontal cortex area, and arrows showing blood supply is *active* in this area. It's lit up because there's more blood flow there and therefore more heat.

The right hand image is of the same person but now they have been given a stimulus that has elicited an anxiety or fear response. If you look, you can see that the brain has reallocated the blood flow to the side of the head, that part that regulates large motor responses – the part of the brain that activates the larger muscles like arms and legs needed for running or punching. You might infer that the brain is gearing up for fight or flight. The brain is also sending hormones like adrenaline and cortisol into the body to be ready to respond and either get out of there, or fight away the danger.

But also notice the blood flow to the part of the brain that usually handles rational thinking and problem solving – the prefrontal cortex – has gone almost!

So you can see that logic doesn't really beat fear. Most people find it hard to think straight when they are in a fear response. Logic can't happen as well when it's actually happening to us, because the part of the brain that controls logic stops working as efficiently.

An MRI scan illustrates this perfectly.

To be fair, the brain is a *better-safe-than-sorry* mechanism programmed to err on the side of keeping us safe.

Why am I telling you this?

A lot of us think that when we're feeling fearful, that it's actually already happening to us. But it's not is it?

What's happening when we're feeling fearful, is that our brain has decided upon the outcome and decided it's – potentially – going to be a bad outcome. Its already asking, *What if...? What if this happens? What if that happens?* This goes with fear.

But that's not actually fear; that's anxiety or worry.

It's the precursor to fear. When something's happening, we're not feeling fearful, we're *getting ready* to get the hell out of there, or fight away. We're dealing with the situation.

Fear lives in the future. It comes from the past, but it lives in the future.

So when you are feeling fearful, you need to take a minute to stop and pause and breathe. And think to yourself: *Is this reality, or is this just my unconscious brain, giving me a shed load of stories and telling me what it's decided the future is going to be?*

This is why this stuff is best done off the horse.

When we are riding the horse, we are having to control the motor functions. Plus horse riding requires adrenaline to deal with all the other stimulants that are going on that we're having to respond to – whilst we're on the horse.

If we want to rewire fear response – which can absolutely, 100%, be done – it needs to be done when we are not in the situation. It also needs to be done if we're going to rewire what we call a *trauma response.*

We have to go into the unconscious – and this is what I do – to play around, with, to change the things that need to be changed, change the stories, change the plans, undo the wiring, and then let it spit it back out again up to your conscious.

Your conscious brain is the gatekeeper.

Even with all the knowledge that I have of this stuff, I have someone that I go to who does that bit for me. I can't do it to myself because the conscious brain is the gatekeeper and getting in the way.

I want you to think about how much of what you call fear is actually fear. How much of it is more worrying about the future and what it might hold?

This is key. If the brain can make it feel *real*, even when you're just thinking about it, it will stop you taking the action.

The brain goes, *Yes, I've won. She didn't take the action, therefore, I can keep her safe. Great. That worked. Brilliant. I shall repeat that.*

That's all the evidence the brain requires. If it works, it repeats it. If it works, it repeats. If it works, it repeats it.

And guess what? If it works, it repeats it, you get good at it. And when you're good at something, we call it a skill. But understand that you can be really skilful at something, even if you don't want to be. You can have a really skilful *fear pattern*.

I'm not saying that this is a dare club. I'm not saying; *feel the fear and do it anyway.* I am saying fear is all in your head; and, it absolutely can be reprogrammed.

The feeling of fear is visceral.

You might say it is real, because your heart rate goes up. Or you sweat, or feel sick. But those things, particularly in the context of us and horse riding, are generally happening *before* the event has happened. Because in the moment when the event is happening, we are dealing with it. Makes sense? And very often our horses respond to something, and then we respond, and then they decide they're definitely must be danger, and then they respond. And then the thing we were worried about *does happen*.

Unconsciously, we're cueing our horse all the time.

Clients typically tell me their fear is about the reaction or response of other people's opinions.

Fear does not have to be about something physical. In fact, most of the time, it's not. Although none of us really want to be falling off, very rarely is the fear about falling off. It's normally about the repercussions after we have fallen off. Things other people think. The stuff other people are going to say to us or about us. That's what it normally is.

So how do you differentiate between fear and danger?

If your fear response is firing so hard that you find even something safe to be scary? How do you decide that you should take that breath or just bale out?

This brings me beautifully on to my next point which is about the difference between fear and trauma response.

Normal, irrational fears — fears that have developed because something happened to us, and then we went, *Oh, I don't want that to happen again, thank you very much.* Or we might have seen it happen to others. When we decide we will do things to keep us safe. The brain organises things to protect bad stuff from happening. Especially *perceived* bad stuff.

But you can overcome that. We use the principle of stretching our comfort zone.

You stretch the comfort zone a little bit, a little bit, a little bit, a little bit... and that becomes a Learning Zone and then eventually, if you stretch it out a little bit, and those learning get embedded, then that becomes your new comfort zone. And then you can do the next bit, which becomes your new comfort zone.

That's how you can stretch yourself to grow, to develop, to learn, to do new things and to do the stuff that once appeared worrying or anxiety inducing to you, you can do it because you've developed the skills required to do it.

However, there is something called trauma.

Now most people think of trauma, as PTSD, or something that happens to people who have had some extreme horrific experience. But trauma lives on a spectrum, and most of us – as horse riders – have experienced some degree of trauma. It doesn't have to be physical; it can be emotional, too.

It is experienced as a trauma because:

- You couldn't get away from it.

- You couldn't access or you didn't have available the skills to do something about it.

- There was a *perceived* risk to life or limb.

And that's the most important part. It's your brain's *perception* – not other people's – but *your* brain's perception. And this is all at the unconscious level.

If you think about it, and you combine those three things, anytime we've had a near miss, or a fall, or we've seen someone else do it, or we've read about it, or we've watched those awful videos where everyone else is falling off, or we've joined some of the Facebook groups where everyone talks about the terrible things that happen to us – particularly the groups that are set up to help you with confidence. In reality, everyone just starts telling each other the stories of why they are the way they are.

And by the way, *your story* is just you justifying why you feel the way you do.

The problem is, the more you tell *your story*, the easier it becomes to tell, the more practiced – or embellished – it becomes in your unconscious brain. And then, the easier it can be to give you the reasons why you shouldn't be doing something.

Trauma is a little bit like a wound made by a thorn.

So for some reason, we end up with a thorn in our arm, and it makes a wound. And it hurts. But rather than remove the thorn – because we don't know how – our brain decides we have to protect ourselves from that thorn getting knocked. So we pad around the thorn. But then it still keeps getting knocked. So we add more padding around it, but it still keeps getting knocked. So then we add more padding around it. And eventually we've got this great big load of padding on top of this wound... that's still got this thorn in it.

And that padding then starts to get in the way of us doing things. It starts to get in the way of us becoming what we want. It starts to get in the way of us trying new stuff, because we're terrified that there might be another thorn that ends up in us. And because it's been such a difficult situation to deal with, naturally, we don't want another one.

That is trauma. And that is coping mechanisms and coping responses. That is what most people think is happening when they're in fear.

But, it's not. It's just your brain protecting you. In that respect, it's created this mechanism and it's gone, *Well, that worked She's not touching the thorn? I don't see the problem.* But is your brain working against you?

But you're going, *True, but I don't want this whole load of padding on my arm.*

And your brains going? *Yeah, but it's working. Like you haven't given me another way. So I'm going to use this one. Thanks.*

So what we need to do is take away the padding, and we need to remove the thorn. So that the wound can heal. Even if it might leave a scar.

Our past experiences are really important to us. But they don't have to have such a huge effect upon our future.

If you find you're constantly trying to do something, but you keep freezing, or it's completely illogical that you're locking up, or you just you just can't get past a certain point – despite trying, despite your best efforts – then we absolutely know that it's because of trauma.

It may be one episode; or it might have been lots of little things that just added up.

And it doesn't have to be physical. It's not only about falling off or hurting yourself or things happening that way. It absolutely can be emotional, too.

Hopefully that helps you, work out the difference between whether you take a breath or bale out. If you are able to look at it logically and go through it and try it again and get over it. Great. If you can't, then it's trauma related.

You need to get that rewired by a professional, which is what we do on Mastermind. The cool part is, its easily accessible and easy to do. And you just need to get in touch and we can speak to you about the options.

What do you think? What's going though your mind right now? Take a moment to capture your insights.

So at this point delegates on the workshops shared:

- I'm not scared of jumping. I'm scared of what could happen. That's not helpful.

- I'm scared of jumping at a show. I freeze up and miscommunicate with my horse. And then he gets scared. And we're both happy to jump over something bigger at home. It's fine. But I can't seem to get to the problem once I'm in the ring.

If it's something that when you're in a competition arena or a ring, that will be something to do with the worry of being judged, or the worry of comparison, or the worry of not being good enough, or imposter syndrome, that kind of stuff. That's all stuff that we can rewire.

- That just triggers a memory. I didn't even think effective. Maybe it all makes sense now.

Sometimes there will be a memory very deep in the unconscious that only this kind of work can bring up. And when I say *this kind of work*, I mean the kind of work we do in our Mastermind programme. Rewiring.

We're not just listening to stories. If there's a story that we're aware of it. But most times we aren't at all aware of what else is stored in there. It doesn't matter either way it can have an effect.

So that's fear. And that's how your brain works with fear; and when a fear response gets triggered. Now would be a great time to note down any insights from this section.

Step 2: Do It

So the next key is *Do it*. *Do it* doesn't mean feel the fear and do it anyway. That's not what it means at all.

It means you need to make sure you're in the right environment, and you're doing the right things – the right behaviours – and that you have you got the right skills and the capabilities.

You need to identify where the fear is coming from. And you possibly need some help to rewire that fear. If there's fear it's coming from somewhere where you can't fix it yourself.

Or you need to start asking the right questions. *Am I doing the right things? Am I putting the right work in to be able to achieve what I want? Am I getting the help I need, now?*

There is absolutely no point intending to do something if you don't have the required skills and the capabilities to execute the desired behaviour. If you don't have the skill and the capability, please don't try and go and do it. Get help.

Now it's possible you might gain a bit of the skill and capability from the experience of trying but, as it relates to riding, it's not really a good thing from a risk assessment perspective, in what is actually a high-risk sport.

What we have to be aware of is all of these things affect each other. The following diagram might help.

MISSION/VISION

IDENTITY

BELIEFS AND VALUES

SKILLS & CAPABILITIES

BEHAVIOURS

ENVIRONMENT

This is psychologist, Robert Dilts' *Neurological Levels*. I believe he created this in collaboration with anthropologist, Gregory Bateson, a linguistics expert who wanted to better understand how people use language to describe and make sense of their experience of reality. Each level is impacted by the level above and below it. But importantly, the effort you focus on the level above, tends to exert greater impact on the level below.

So while your *environment* affects your *behavior,* your *behaviour* has a greater impact on your *environment*. Or can. And should.

This might seem counterintuitive especially if you believe that you are a victim of circumstances and what shows up in your world.

Riding well – or not – occurs in your environment.

What alters your ability to ride well, is a result of your *behaviour.* If you are struggling to ride well, it is indicating the need to develop skills, not continue to master riding badly! What shapes your ability to ride well are your *skills and capabilities.*

But what shapes your skills? The *belief* that you can ride well. Belief determines what is important to you. Critically, that it is possible for you improve your skills... so that you ride well (or that we could observe you applying those skills)... and what shows up in the environment is *good horse riding.*

Note: Your skills and capabilities indicate what you *believe* you can and can't do. When you say *I can't...* you are making a statement of belief. The word *can* is a permissive verb, so when you say, *I can't...* you are really saying *I won't give myself permission to.*

It begs the question, *Why not?* The answer usually starts with, *Because...* which also indicates its a belief issue, not a skills issue. (Can you see now why it's not your horse, or the yard, or the kit (environment) that is at fault? And why it is pointless trying to engineer your environment for something that requires an intervention at the skills or belief level?)

Above *belief* sits *identity.* If you say to yourself, *I am a good rider* or *I am a good learner and I believe can learn and apply good skills.* All those *I am* affirmations flow from positive identity statements.

If you say, *I am a bad rider...* or *I am rubbish at riding...* that indicates a negative identity mindset.

But above that sits *mission and vision* – or intentionality. Basically, I intend to ride well.

Most of the changes you want to make in riding – and your life – are better made at the top three levels. But I just want to look at the bottom three for a minute.

Most of the time, we are working on skills, behaviours and environment. Most training or education that you have done was delivered across these three levels.

This is logic. This is the conscious brain arena. Typically, you are trying to change your mindset from the bottom up.

The environment is all about what you can see and hear around you. What shows up. It impacts your behaviours – what you are doing or saying and what others are doing or saying. What we can observe happening.

And skills: are you learning and improving; or getting better at or worse at?

The top three levels are more the domain of the unconscious brain. This is where our beliefs live – what's important to us; and what we believe we fear. And above that who we think we are. *Who am I as a person? And above that what do I want anyway? What is what is it all about for me? What do I want? Where do I want to be?* This is where your dreams and your goals live. Your mission and vision. The bigger picture stuff.

I can give you riding lessons - skills behaviours, environment stuff – but changing mindset is delivered top down from your intentions, identity and beliefs.

Where you need to change becomes obvious.

Decide what it is that you want to do. Who you want to be. What you believe is true. Which will inform the skills you acquire, your behaviours and ultimately how you ride.

If you want to be better at something, then you need to improve your skills and your capabilities so that when you sit in the saddle, life is different

But mindset change occurs when you're not in the saddle, as well.

For most people they don't understand the necessity to start with the mission/vision, identity and beliefs and values parts.

- What's important to me and why?

- What can I do?

- What can I/can't I do?

- What's possible? What's not possible?

- What do I think about the world around me?

- What rules do I have in place?

- Which ones am I living by?

- Which ones are getting in the way?

- Which one to help me along?

This is really important to understand. Of course, it's about developing skills, it's about behaviour change and taking action. No argument. But for rapid, smoother change its about dreaming bigger, deciding on you identity – who you want to be, and noticing whether your beliefs align with the skills you want to acquire and the behaviours you want to demonstrate.

Do you agree with that? What are your thoughts and experiences on that? Please take a moment to reread this chapter. Figure out where you need the most help. But also identify where the most help can be delivered.

Fear Stops You Taking Action

This book is ultimately about action. And fear stops action. But why? Why does fear stop action?

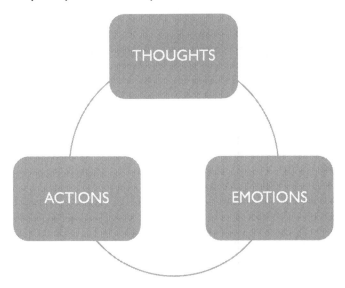

Our thoughts – which are comprised of internal pictures and sounds and words in our heads – affect our emotions. Every thought we have has an emotion attached to it, because that's how the unconscious brain works. It puts things together, it makes associations. And it does them in pictures and emotions and feelings.

And then every emotion we have drives whether or not we take action.

If you think, *I'm going to go for a ride today,* a picture will come into your head or maybe some words – or both. And if you think, *It's going to be a lovely ride today,* you'll probably imagine sunshine, You'll see it going well. You will see yourself having a lovely time with your horse. That creates nice, happy, excited emotions.

So you'll go and do it. Or at least take the first action to get towards doing it.

Which then means if it goes well, that adds to those stories – that story bank that you have in your head about riding – and what that subsequently means. You feel good about it, and therefore you do more of it.

That's the positive cycle. That's the one we want. That's the one that builds confidence. It's is the one that builds more action, because thoughts and emotions drive action.

But if you think about the flip side of it, if you think, *I'm going to go for a ride... and it's all going to go wrong... and my horse is going to misbehave... because it did it before... and I don't think it's going to be very nice... and I don't think it's going to go well...* and all the emotions that come with that will come with all the negativity, plus all of the fear, the worry, the anxiety, plus all of the unhappy emotions, then you're less likely to do it.

And then you are more likely to make excuses.

So remember earlier when I asked, *Are you the perfect excuse maker?* This is where they come from.

Oh, well, I can't do that today because my leg is slightly less happy than it normally is. So I can't possibly do it. Or, *Well, I don't actually have as much time as I thought I did now.* Or , *Well I couldn't find one of my horses boots. And it can't possibly go without those boots.*

Look, my friend isn't able to now never mind, that means I can't go. And I'm no good as a rider anyway... and what if...

All this weird, wonderful stuff we come up with.

And then funnily enough, we don't do it. So then the thoughts that come into our head, *Oh look, I'm alive. And I didn't go and it's OK. So that's all right, then, isn't it?*

And this is the cycle that we need to be aware of.

This is also the *What-If* cycle. *What if that happens?*

The *what-ifs* are our anxious thoughts – pictures and words – and feelings.

So if you're thinking, *What if it goes wrong? What if this bad thing happens?* You have to stop yourself.

And then you have to say, *What if it goes well? What if it's good? What if it actually turns out the way I'd like it to?* This is the ability to future pace it going right, rather than going wrong.

But can you *consciously* stop yourself? And you can do this easily? When you find yourself doing the *what-ifs* you say this word. It works really well.

Stop!

That word interrupts the pattern that your brain is in. *What? Stop! You heard. Stop* is a circuit breaker word.

And then you could ask, *What if it's good? What if it goes well? What if I can create positive emotions that create a different action?*

It's the same cycle. Just positive.

Thoughts create emotions, which create actions (which creates a response in our horse), which creates our thoughts and our emotions and our actions. You can see how left to run wild how you end up in a negative downward spiral.

Especially, if we add in a few of the negative thoughts like, *Don't spook at that. Don't do that. Don't fall off. Don't do this.*

What happens? Our horse spooks. We fall off. And there we go. Our self-fulfilling prophecy of, *I knew it was going to happen.*

Here's the deal. Your unconscious brain cannot process negatives.

If I'd asked you what your goal was, at the beginning of this book, you probably have been able to tell me, *I want to be able to go and do X... without Y happening.*

Remember earlier on we said your conscious mind is the *goal setter?* And your unconscious mind is the *goal getter?*

If you have a negative spin on what you want; if you are focusing on what you don't want, all your unconscious mind can do is focus on... what you don't want.

If I say to you, right now, don't think of a purple chicken... whatever you do, don't think of a purple chicken... don't think of a purple chicken... don't think of a purple chicken... you'll be thinking, *I can't stop thinking of a purple chicken.*

Or you might have done something weird and wonderful, like made it yellow, or change it into a cow or something.

But essentially, your brain had to think of the purple chicken, first. It then had to *stop* thinking of it. It then had to check whether it was thinking of it, which means it needed to think of it in order to then try and stop thinking of it. But then it had to check it wasn't thinking of it. And basically all you end up doing is thinking of it. This is how negative emotions work.

But you can't process a negative.

Your unconscious brain has something called filters set to it. And what happens is it filters out the information it thinks is relevant, and it allows in the information it thinks is relevant. This is why your unconscious brain is very good at the *how*.

So if you're filling it with *I don't want this, I don't want that,* and *I don't want this to happen...* then that's all it can think about. It will go and find the things relevant to that. It can't do negatives like *don't.*

A friend of mine is a trainer, who was working with a rider who was trying to go slowly for the vara pick up (in working equitation) and she was saying to herself, *Not fast canter, not fast canter, not fast canter...* and she said, *All very well and good, but your horse doesn't hear the NOT part.*

Likewise, your brain doesn't hear the NOT part. All it hears is *fast canter, fast canter.*

That's really important. Make sure that you turn it around and think, *OK, this is the rhythm of the canter that I want...* rather than thinking about what you don't want.

When we're riding our horses, we are giving them unconscious cues. We're getting a little bit tense or a little bit tighter in our hands, or our breathing changes, our heart rates gone up.

If we once had a stop at a trakehner jump for what could be a huge number of reasons then our horse is picking up on this. But our horse doesn't think, *Oh, it's OK It's because we are doing cross country and that is a trakehner jump. That's why her heart rates up it's not a problem. It's all right. That's why she's reacting this way.*

The horse thinks, *Oh, that must be danger. It must be danger. Oh, it's that jump with a ditch again! Do you know every time that ditch jump thing appears she does this danger signal stuff? Well, I think I'll stop then because it must be scary. And I'll look in the ditch at the bottom of the trakehner, because she is staring in it too.*

Then the danger signals stop for a bit. And then the rider gets convinced that their horse has a problem with a trakehener jump!

We now know it *doesn't* actually have a problem with it at all. What's happened is the rider has unconsciously cued the horse. That is the issue.

The horse experiences, *There must be an issue...* and did the same behavior again because the rider cued it. It then gets worse the more it is practised.

Do you realise that you do that?

That's now going to change. We're going to make sure that all your thoughts are set in what we call the positive frame.

So what do you want?

Someone recently asked me:

- I have a young horse and I can definitely get caught in a spiral of *what-ifs* and it's probably the thing that holds me back the most. Do you have any tips to quiet down the negative thoughts?

Here is the simple answer.

Stop. Focus on what you *do* want. Focus on what you do want all the time. Picture it, say it, feel it, focus on it all the time. Journal on it. Write it. This is all stuff that you can do consciously that starts to rewire and respond in the right direction.

Catch them and reverse them.

It's a big topic but I've given you some small tools that you can do now, today that will have a positive impact.

People say, *Give me the advanced stuff!* I can give you all the advanced tools but if you won't apply the small tools – that work – what makes me think you will action the advance techniques?

Put what's in this book into action. Prove it to yourself. Then let's talk advanced stuff.

Logic doesn't beat fear. Logic doesn't undo trauma. Logic doesn't change the wiring in your brain, the patterning and what's going on.

It absolutely can do some things to start making some changes, but if you're thinking, *I've tried all this stuff, and it hasn't worked,* then that's because what you most likely need is some rewiring. (We cover rewiring in Mastermind.)

Start here. The tools in this book are an great place to start. Remember baby steps?

OK, your thoughts and insights? Keep notes, and each time you've done something, even if it's something really tiny and simple and seems small, when you're having a bad day, if you go back and look at it, you'll suddenly realise how many steps you've achieved even if they're small ones to get to your goal. That will give you the encouragement then to push that last bit rather than giving up.

This is why our Performance Journals are available on the website so that you can keep track each day of what went well, what needs to change and how you will take action to change it. This then adds up to weekly and monthly goals and reflections. It all helps you to see your progress and spot patterns too.

Step 3: Love It

Loving it is about *genuinely* wanting to do more. It's about wanting to take the next step. It's about knowing that it might be hard, but still wanting it enough to say, *OK, I'm gonna overcome that.*

It's about being motivated towards what you *do* want.

Pain causes most of our actions. I don't necessarily mean physical pain; I mean emotional pain as well. When we're not happy about something.

How many people absolutely don't go to the dentist, but if they had a tooth problem, and if they have really, really bad toothache, suddenly, they would find time to make that appointment and go. That's actual pain, but pain drives action. Our environment – the toothache – is booking the appointment. Pain drives more than pleasure.

But the problem is if we're always motivated *away from* pain all the time – so we're always running from what we *don't* want. We don't want to feel a failure. We don't want to feel like others are judging us. We don't want to feel like we're not making any progress. We don't want to feel not good enough – all of that stuff. If we're just running from what we don't want we're shooting arrows and hoping they hit somewhere.

But what we want to do is laser focus those arrows, which is why I say, set the goal, set the intention... then you get your target.

You might not know at this point how to shoot an arrow, but your motivation is that target and obviously in the inertia of that you'll be getting away from the other things.

So we need to make sure that we're always motivated the way that we want to be.

And it's about that motivation. What is this all about for you? I had to assess my own motivation , when my scores were going really badly. My mare didn't really like me and when things were really hard I'd ask, *Why am I even doing this? Why am I working so hard?*

And the answer that came back was: *To pay for your horse!*

And I thought, *This is crazy. Surely I can flip this one around.*

So I did. I set up my own business. That means I've got time to spend with my horses. I'm doing what I love and now I'm massively motivated to grow this business even further than it already has to help even more people all round the world.

Why are you motivated to ride?

It is a bit of a mad sport, isn't it? When we think about it, we're on the back of a half ton animal with its own ideas, asking it to do things that sometimes it doesn't really want to do. And we're expecting it to join in with us and go along with it.

And we're all a little bit insane, aren't we?

So why do you ride? What's it all about? The lifestyle not just the riding? There is definitely a whole lifestyle around riding, particularly if your horse owner. It's not just about the riding.

So what is it about that lifestyle? The partnership? Absolutely. When you get that moment when actually you feel like you are in it *together;* when you are in harmony together.

How amazing is that moment? When you feel like you're both doing it because you both want to? You need to look at these things and constantly assess them.

Loving it is about motivation. It's about knowing our why.

Emotions

Emotions drive our WHY. How are your emotions involved? What emotions are you driven by? What emotions do you want more of? You get the rewiring and you do what you need.

When it comes to motivation, we're all *happy hormone* junkies. There are actually four happy hormones: dopamine, oxytocin, serotonin and endorphins. And when we do anything that gives us one of those hormones, we feel good.

Horse riding gives you a dopamine hit. Dopamine is the *feel good* hormone that kicks in when you feel some pain – but also a high – without it you would never persist. But dopamine makes us think we want to do it again.

If we consider the hobby of horse riding (and the business of it, too) we can understand why we become so passionate about them and it creates a whole lifestyle around them. They actually do tick off all of the four happy hormones…

1. **Dopamine:** Feelings of wellbeing are a primary driver of the brain's reward system and it spikes when we experience something pleasurable. Getting affection from your horse? Your dopamine levels will go up fast. Praised by your trainer? You'll get a big dopamine hit. Completing the Cross Country? Massive surge of it. It basically links any enjoyable activity with a feeling of a high.

2. **Serotonin:** Exercise and spending time outdoors can help boost serotonin. These are two primary parts of being around horses, especially riding them. Serotonin plays a key role in keeping anxiety and depression at bay and why it is often called the *feel good* hormone.

3. **Endorphins:** Again, these are mostly linked to exercise. Which we will get from either riding or caring for horses in some way. These are very powerful hormones and actually act as painkillers. They are the key reason that we can push through pain in times of pressure or necessity, especially in sport. This is what we hear as a *runners high* and often is what eventers, show jumpers and those who go riding fast across the country get for instance.

4. **Oxytocin:** Often referred to as the *love hormone*. We get a rush of this when we cuddle, stroke or touch animals (as well as humans). When we are with horses (especially when riding them and feeling in harmony) we get this hormone released as it is best known for its role in bonding and attachment in mothers with their babies.

So it probably comes as no surprise that having a passion for horses can feel like an incurable addiction. Which is why we ignore fear, anxiety and the risks involved in order to keep on being around them.

What about adrenaline junkies?

Adrenaline junkies just have to be on the edge all the time. They spike the cortisol and adrenaline which that allows the creation of these happy hormones when they dissipate. They have to push themselves out into panic or stress (well beyond comfort or learning) so they have to do more and more extreme things to get it.

And it is literally *junky*. It is an addiction.

What adrenaline junkies love, is the adrenaline and the cortisol that is released through doing something that's about to give you fear. But nine times out of ten, they have done enough of an assessment that the unconscious brain is going, *Yeah, I love the adrenaline, I love the adrenaline, but actually, we're going to be fine, I truly believe will actually be fine.*

So they still do it.

Adrenaline junkies do not believe their sport is going to kill them. They believe there's a chance it will. And that's what gives them the adrenaline.

We don't need to become adrenaline junkies in order to enjoy ourselves with horses. We can push ourselves outside of our comfort zone to progress without needing to go anywhere near stress or panic.

Each time we do something that feels good and releases any of the four happy hormones, we then are motivated to want to do more of it.

A Small Step Every Day
Adds Up To Big Results

Look at this picture for a moment.

When we set actions, we need to set ourselves up for success. Make them tiny, achievable and trackable. Make them small enough to feel almost easy and then keep repeating them, assessing them and pushing them. Bit by bit. Because it is when we don't do this that we don't get the hit of hormones and instead start to feel demotivated and overwhelmed.

Start to think about how you can harness the power of your brain and body and make it work for you. It is far better to complete lots of tiny little steps than it is to go for the big ones and fail.

Take a moment to think about something you currently feel overwhelmed with. Are you seeing it as one big chunk of things beyond your control? Does it seem too big to tackle? Are you avoiding it?

Now break it down. What is one tiny step you can make? What is one thing that is within your control? What is one thing you can do that will bring you some joy? That will release some happy hormones again?

Assessment

It's also about being OK with checking in on things, assessing stuff; deciding if it's right for us; deciding if that's the action we want to be taking; deciding where that's going to take us to looking at the action, analyzing it.

That's important. Keep adjusting.

I worry about getting the stride wrong on the approach to each fence. On approach I ask am I in a good canter, I'm in the right rhythm, I'm on a good stride? How do keep going and not get distracted by the questions? This can then affect my motivation because I over analyse and beat myself up.

So much of riding is actually about what we *feel* but we think it is about systems and logic.

When we *think* we're going to miss a stride it is because we are probably trying to use sight and proprioception to gauge the take off and anticipate it. Our body takes over whatever patterns it has learnt in the past.

I actually did my Master's project on seeing stride and debunked this myth. It's got nothing to do with sight, whatsoever.

I had to work with four top showjumpers and four people who were OK at jumping. I picked riding club level people.

It turns out the riding club people were *convinced* they could see a stride and the top showjumpers actually just *felt* the canter. I had to get into the unconscious mind of the top showjumpers. They had so much that they just did without knowing consciously how or why they did it. I had to really get into their brains and ask them a load of questions – in a certain way – to help them realise their strategy. I couldn't guide them; it had to come from them.

When I looked at the pattern between the four of them, they knew exactly what a good twelve-foot canter *felt* like on that horse that they were riding. Some horses are short, and they're going to get in more strides. Some horses are bigger and longer and rangier so, they're going to get in less. But the riders had this *way* of being able to tell.

You need to work – not on *seeing* the stride – but *feeling* it.

In addition, the top showjumpers *didn't* anticipate the horse... or the stride... or the takeoff. They literally waited until they had that moment when the horse moved its weight onto the forehand, a fraction, to be able to bring it back and up. It was at that point, they knew they were going to take off; that they were then ready to go with the horse.

So that's the other thing. They didn't interfere. They let the horse make the decision – to whatever degree. The better at it they got the more often they could get that shot bang-on, and they really didn't need to interfere with the horse because they've got it right.

The horse could then just do it using its own proprioception.

The point is that so much of our learning is unconscious and with horses it is hugely about *feel*. When we try to over-intellectualise it in the moment we are in our conscious brain and we need to spend time allowing ourselves to feel more in the moment and then go back and reflect an analyse afterwards when it isn't occupied with the doing.

This is why great coaches stop us and reflect on what we have just done rather than just keep shouting the same instructions at us when we are riding. Then they allow us to work out what was good, what can be improved ad how to do it.

A study was done on the difference between the *self-talk* of professional riders and the self-talk of grass roots riders, whilst warming up for a dressage competition.

Both sets of riders where given microphones and voice recorders. They were told to say out loud *anything* they were thinking.

The recordings were then analysed.

The pro-riders said a lot of *good, more, less, no, yes* etc. They were internally assessing and making adjustments. The grass roots riders had a lot more verbose inner dialogue with themselves. They would say, *I'm good at this..., We struggle with x..., Oh no I forgot to do y again..., This was better on z day..., Why wont you do a, b,c"* etc.

Their comments were a lot more self-judgemental rather than analytical. They were far more driven by emotion and associations.

They also were less able to analyse the test they later rode in terms of what needed to be improved and more able to give it an overall judgement of whether they were happy or disappointed with it. They were understandably more concerned with whether they had enjoyed the test and outcome.

The pro-riders where able to look analytically at what happened and make actionable steps to improve, change, or learn something that was missing. No surprise that they were more concerned with seeing the test as a part of their job to improve the horse and developed the learning of both the partnership.

Fun wasn't really an aspect.

Is This Fun?

A question to keep asking yourself is:

Is this fun?

Now, I'm not going to say that to get to a big goal, a big dream, it's always going to be fun. But if you are a leisure rider, and this is a hobby it really would be better if it was mostly fun, right? If you are a pro-rider, you can have fun, too. How amazing would that be? You're doing what you love.

So you can have fun.

A great question to constantly be assessing yourself is, *Is this fun?* And it might be that in that moment, it's not. And that's OK.

And you just assess it and you take a moment and think, *OK, what can I do to change that? I love accomplishing the bond with the horse and achieving what I want out of the training and progressing the horse and myself.*

It's really common that something that we really value here is progression, development, partnership, achievement, they're really important to horse riders, they are definitely things that I have discovered over the years are important values to horse riders.

We get really upset and annoyed when actually those things aren't happening.

That's, part of doing something that pushes you out your comfort zone, isn't it? You're not just doing the same thing every time you want achievement.

But what's achievement?

Achievement is when we feel we have progressed, moved forward or accomplished a goal. And that can be a mini goal. That can be a tiny micro goal. It doesn't have to be a big one.

For instance, it could be the mini goal if I kept my hands still. If I stayed aware as I jumped that jump. If I kept looking up. If I relaxed my bum cheeks, as I used my leg.

So they are mini goals. Incremental gains.

And they're really, really, really important to achieve in the big goals. It's all the little mini ones *tick, tick, tick, tick,* as we get them. In comes a dopamine junkie, *tick, tick, tick, tick, tick* on the mini goal, *tick, tick, tick, tick, tick* on the mini goal.

Every time we get a tick, the dopamine comes in, and so we think, *Yes, brilliant. I love this.*

Anything that involves skill, we only develop skills and get better at skills by doing them. And again, we don't want to get better, at the skills we don't want.

So we have to continuously be assessing our skills, don't we? We have to be continuously thinking, *Was that how I wanted it to be? Was that helpful? Did that get me closer towards what I wanted? Is that something I want to do? Again? What was good about that? What was not good about that?*

And we need that continuous assessment, not only in our physical skills, but in our mindset as well.

Keep assessing and adjusting. That helps you to keep on track towards your goal and also, to keep enjoying the journey of progress.

By tracking, you can see if you have gone a bit off the pathway. If you are enjoying the detour, then great. If not, you might want to assess what we can do to get that enjoyment back again.

Part 2

Support Moving Forward

Support

Support is something that fundamentally, we all need as human beings. We started as tribes people. We were nomads. They say we were cavemen who lived in caves, but we were actually nomads that wandered around. We were built to roam. But together.

The men went off to hunt and the women gathered. And the women supported each other, nurtured each other. We had children and raised children in tribes. But we did it together.

Like all mammals, we are social animals. We give and receive help. Because you can't do everything on your own. We come from tribes. Tribal life was important. We are hardwired to look after each other.

And we need support. We need people around us. We cannot do everything on our own. We need nurturing. We need help with things. We need people to go and do stuff for us. We need to do stuff for others.

And despite the Industrial Revolution, and the rapid changes in technology especially in the last fifty years, that have suggested we can go it alone, we are still wired for connection.

We can't do everything on our own. We think we can, but we can't. Yes, we can survive on our own – go out and buy food –

but that still requires people. It still requires people to grow, harvest, package and deliver the food.

You can survive on a desert island. But survival is a very different thing. Survival is literally staying alive and doing whatever is necessary to preserve life. But you do not just want to survive. You want to thrive.

We want to enjoy life. We want to dream it, do it and love it. But we need support doing that, too. We all need physical, emotional, and mental support.

This is one of my favourite pictures to show the sort of support I'm talking about. They are all supporting someone else, and all feel supported – just not all at the same time.

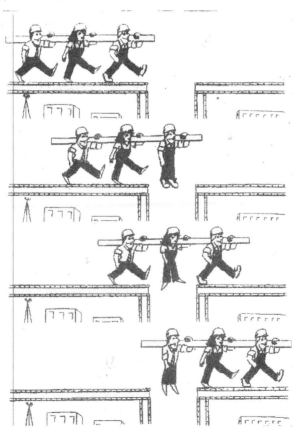

When you think about support, who do you need? What support do you need? And right now, how much do you feel supported?

On a scale of one to ten – zero being nothing at all and ten being perfect, how supported do you feel?

- What do you score yourself as far as your physical well being?
- How much did you score yourself in as far as your mental well being?
- And how do you rate yourself on the emotional support scale?

If so if you're scoring perfect tens then that's amazing – not statistically normal – but if you feel that supported can you tell me your secret?

That might mean at some point in time, you're going to need the support of the people around you.

My saddler speaks to my horse physio. I share the reports of the body worker to them both. My trainer, watches what the saddler does and my physio talks to my trainer. They are individuals but they work together on my team.

I work with trainers a lot. A trainer will ask, *Can you help this client?* We get the client booked on to the Mastermind. I then encourage the client to share their learning from Mastermind with their trainer so they can understand what is going on a bit more. The trainer is normally thrilled when the client gets rid of whatever was mentally holding them back. It frees them up to apply their expertise to help improve the clients' physical skills again.

If you look at Flying Changes Mindset, we've got a team of Ambassadors. They pull together as a team, they sort each other's issues out before I even know they happened, which is great.

They pull together as a team, because they know I'm doing my part, which is helping as many people as I can, and helping them individually if needed. They help each other out and then we all grow. There's a saying: *All ships rise on a rising tide.*

Everyone benefits.

But if there's a competition and oneupmanship, there's trying to be better than others.

I understand competition. When we go to compete, we want to do the best we can and compete. But that doesn't mean doing that by treading on someone else. Or doing that by being nasty towards someone else. Or by psyching someone else out or saying horrible things. We don't have to do it that way.

You can do it by being the best you can. If we all try and be the best we can then everyone benefits. And so do our horses.

The best example is support at the elite athletes level. They have a team that work together as a team.

Athletes at the top level, know they didn't get there on their own. They will have ridden the horse, of course. But they had a whole team of grooms, saddlers, farriers, feed experts, trainers, mindset experts etc.

They've got sponsors and backers. They've got their family, the people that help run the place, a host of people behind them. You just see them out there doing the job. It looks like just them but its not. They have a team that work together as a team.

They recognise when they need help. More so at the elite level, they ask for help and support as and when they need it.

I am a high-performance mindset coach. And I might be the highest level that you can be trained in to do what I do, in fact I can train others all the way to the top levels, too. But I still have a mindset coach. Because there's a whole load of unconscious stuff that goes on for me that I can't know about, because it's unconscious.

And as much time as I can spend exploring it, I still need someone else to sometimes go in there and sort it for me.

Everyone needs support.

So, is it OK for you to ask for support?

Power Questions

I want you to think about these power questions.

These questions require you to think about what you've read.

- What have you got from this book so far?

- What can you start, do, or use?

- What can you start doing right now?

- What do you need to stop doing?

- What do you need to continue doing?

- What positive decisions are you already making now?

Please stop and make some notes.

What Are You Going To Start Doing?

Improving your performance requires changing something. To change anything you need to:

- Stop doing something unresourceful that doesn't work for you.

- Start doing something resourceful that works for you.

- Continue doing whatever is working.

Typically, clients say:

- I'm going to stop the *what-ifs* and start building what I can do with my gorgeous mare after three years on and off of injuries.

- I'm going to start asking myself better questions and I'm already feeling there are ways I can use this in my professional life too.

Do you know what the theme of this book is? This is all mindset work. What you apply it to is entirely up to you.

Now obviously I made everything applicable to riding. But my clients apply those strategies to other areas of their life.

I had one lady that joined the course because she wanted some help with skiing. And I have a lot of people that found the tools in this book helped them to understand and improve stuff going on in their relationships, their business, their health, their careers.

When you understand your brain you can apply it to whatever you want. On workshops, delegates say:

- I'm going to flip the *can'ts* and *don'ts* into *how do I love it?*

- I'm going to remember it's fun. It's a big thing to do.

- I'm going to say stop where my mindset is focusing on all things that could go wrong, and try and change that to a nice, easy, successful lesson that always is brilliant.

Now it's your turn.

Next Steps

I want to tell you about how we can support you going forward. If you've found this really interesting; if this has been a tantalizing taster, and you've got a million and one questions, and you want the journey to continue, then great.

Here are four current options for moving forwards.

The Inner Circle

The *Inner Circle* is my premier coaching and training package and currently the only way you can get one-to-one coaching with me.

As part of the *Inner Circle* you are invited to join me on a gorgeous luxury body and mind retreat, where we get together and dig about unrooting the much deeper brain stuff that we can only really do in-person, to get the total transformation.

We spend time working on not only your mind but also getting you aware of your body too, including a spa treatment or two and all in a beautiful rural location, in luxury accommodation, usually a hot tub, with good food and lots of great memories.

You get a monthly group call as well, in the *Inner Circle* and everything that's in Mastermind too.

You also get access to all the online mini courses scheduled during the year – all included.

You also you get VIP tickets to our special in-person clinics and events.

So if you're thinking you'd love to go for it I can assure you that I will have your back all the way. The *Inner Circle* is designed to look at whatever it is that you need to get to, wherever it is you want to go to.

Please contact me on the link below.

www.contactjenni.me

If you want to book an Action Plan call with me to have a chat about it – no obligation – then you can absolutely do that using this link.

Mastermind Group (Zoom)

Mastermind is a weekly group coaching program. It's twelve parts, over three months. We deep dive into twelve key topics during that time as a group. We really focus on the brain rewiring technique and do demonstrations and hot-seat breakthrough sessions via Zoom.

While they are done as a group you don't have to share anything. I don't need to know what your story is. I've done thousands of one-to-ones so we are able to do the rewiring rapidly.

When I'm doing these sessions your unconscious brain is doing its thing and I'm guiding you through it. You do not have to tell anyone anything about what's going on for you, which is great, because it also means where they're not sharing horror stories with each other, as well.

There's an online exclusive member's area where you can chat and share things. And it's a really great group.

You also get access to the Online Learning Zone, which is where we put a lot of invaluable theory resources.

You get accountability groups; groups where you get together and share how you are doing. *Are you any closer or not? What do you need to do to get there? What's going on for you? What is it that's holding you back? Do you need to go and do one of the sessions that we might have done another time?*

You have access to me via Messenger.

You do actually get one hour 1-2-1 at the end of Mastermind day, where we check in with what progress you've made.

You get a ninety-day journal.

You get online treats and goodies via the group.

You get the community.

Plus it's super easy for anyone to access anywhere in the world.

It really is an amazing program. And it's been absolutely unbelievable the things that the members have achieved as a result of Mastermind. If you'd like to know more and receive direct links go to *www.contactjenni.me*

Dream It Into Life

Dream It Into Life is a powerful six-part online course. We expand on the three *Dream It, Do It, Love It* steps.and cover:

- Our goals and plans and what stops them happening.

- Detailed causes of fear and how to overcome it.

- What starts and stops the actions and reversing those what-ifs in more detail. So you take action, and then gain an understanding of skills analysis and feedback loops, rebooting your dream and reassessing them. So if you had a dream, and you sacked it off, but actually you want to reignite it again, we will look into that as well.

- And then also taking your first steps towards making your dreams a reality.

You also get a workbook to go alongside the course. To sign up and access the course go to this link

www.contactjenni.me

Please do take one minute right now to join us in the free Empowered Questions community, which is our Facebook Group. You can join right now at

https://www.facebook.com/groups/605562209948466

Or simply search for Empowered Equestrians Community in Facebook Groups.

In this group, I go live in the mornings with my dog, The Spru, while I'm out walking him, to talk about all sorts of topics that are relevant to people. Loads of people love hearing these lives. And they've helped so many people with things because I just talk about things that come up and share those.

Links and Resources

You can download the latest resources and find out everything about our programs and events by simply going to

www.contactjenni.me

DREAM IT DO IT LOVE IT

Acknowledgments

Firstly this book would not have been possible if it wasn't for Andrew Priestley, my business coach and publisher, giving me the push to actually write it, fast!

Even before that, I got my first taste of becoming an international bestselling author thanks to Sammy Blindell who encouraged me to be a contributing author in The Law of Brand Attraction 2.

There have been a huge number of teachers and mentors in my life who have contributed to this book becoming something that came out of my own head. Particularly of note are a few who were catalysts of change for me -

My NLP Trainer, Reg Connelly, gave me the initial knowledge and skills in brain rewiring and gently nudged me in the right directions to become an NLP Master and eventually Trainer, too.

Elaine Wilkins, I have to say thank you to you because you are my guardian Angel, without whom I would never have left that corporate job to pursue my passion.

Jennifer Louise, my conference wifey who was my cheerleader when things got tough in business and my inspiration throughout the pandemic – to come out the other side stronger and in a position to make this book happen.

Finally, my Marketing team, Alice and Charlotte of *Herd It Here Creative,* who put up with my crazy entrepreneurial changes of direction and just carry on doing what they do best to promote whatever project I'm on now.

This time round it was a book!

About Jenni Winter-Leach

Nurturing individuals and their talent have always been at the heart of Jenni Winter-Leach's professional life. After enjoying a successful corporate career as a Global Consultant in Talent Management, Jenni felt the need to combine her love for the equestrian world and her ability as a performance coach. This led her to develop *Flying*  *Changes Mindset,* a market-leading business in the equestrian sphere and the UK's largest equestrian mindset training and coaching company.

As an International Master Mindset and Performance Psychology Coach and Trainer, award-winning professional speaker and international bestselling author, Jenni trains riders at ALL levels of equestrian sport to develop their mental performance and create real and lasting impacts on their enjoyment and results. Jenni also coaches and supports Instructors and Trainers to continue delivering her methods after she has left.

Using unique methods developed as a result of years of training and experience and an extensive toolkit of proven strategies, Jenni has helped many riders improve their mental strength, overcome fears, perform at their very best and consistently achieve improved results and enjoyment. By creating her programmes to suit a rider's unique needs, Jenni is able to ensure that every individual she works with achieves their own unique goals in an efficient, effective and sustainable way.

Contact Jenni Winter-Leach

www.contactjenni.me

Printed in Great Britain
by Amazon